ASPECTS OF P.E.

HOW SPORT IS ORGANIZED

Kirk Bizley

Heinemann
LIBRARY

To Louise

First published in Great Britain by Heinemann Library
Halley Court, Jordan Hill, Oxford OX2 8EJ,
a division of Reed Educational & Professional Publishing Ltd.

Heinemann is a registered trademark of Reed Educational & Professional Publishing Ltd.

OXFORD FLORENCE PRAGUE MADRID ATHENS
MELBOURNE AUCKLAND KUALA LUMPUR SINGAPORE TOKYO
IBADAN NAIROBI KAMPALA JOHANNESBURG GABORONE
PORTSMOUTH NH (USA) CHICAGO MEXICO CITY SAO PAULO

Designed by Celia Floyd

Printed and bound in Italy by L.E.G.O.

01 00 99 98 97
10 9 8 7 6 5 4 3 2 1

ISBN 0 431 07496 8

British Library Cataloguing in Publication Data

Bizley, Kirk
    How Sport is Organized. — (Aspects of P.E.)
    1. Sports administration
    I. Title
    796'.069

Acknowledgements

The Publishers would like to thank the following for permission to reproduce photographs: Action
Plus/Glynn Kirk p21; Allsport pp11, 37; Allsport/Al Bello p43; Allsport/Bob Martin p18;
Allsport/Mike Hewitt pp15, 32; Allsport/Pascal Rondeau p26; Colorsport p41; Dee Conway p31;
Empics/Tony Marshall p22; Image Bank/Becker p19; J Allan Cash Ltd pp4, 30; Kos Picture
Source/Peter Danby p27; Meg Sullivan pp5, 8, 9, 14, 20; Mike Brett Photography pp6, 24; National
Coaching Federation pp25, 29; Oxford Brookes University Sport p28; Rex Features p7; Sporting
Pictures (UK) Ltd p40; The Hulton-Deutsch Collection p38; The Hutchison Library p34

Cover photograph reproduced with permission of Kos Picture Source/Peter Danby

The author and publisher would like to thank Nuala Mullan and Doug Neate for their comments
in the preparation of this book.

Our thanks to Oxford Brookes University Sport and Oxford City Rugby Club for their assistance
during photo shoots.

Every effort has been made to contact copyright holders of any material reproduced in this book.
Any omissions will be rectified in subsequent printings if notice is given to the Publisher.

796.069
312

Contents

Words in **bold** in text are explained in the glossary on page 46

Sport is organized at many different levels to match the standard at which any player may be taking part. Many sports-people you can think of will probably have competed at:

- local level (for a school team or something similar)

- regional level (for an area team or even a county team)

- national level (in national championships)

- international level (representing their country against other countries).

The organization involved at these different levels is quite considerable. Without the proper backing, no one would be able to compete at all of these different standards. Clubs, **local authorities**, schools and national **governing bodies** all play their part.

Running a club: the people

From the most basic level to the highest, clubs have a particular structure which they follow, so that they can run efficiently and enable sport to take place. Not all clubs are **professional**, run by people who are paid to work for them full-time. Many of them, especially at the lower levels, are run by volunteers who do all of the work in their spare time. They each have particular jobs to do.

In almost any club, the following people would be taking responsibilities:

- The **chairperson** has overall control of the club and runs the meetings which the club would regularly hold. These meetings are governed by a set of rules called the club's **constitution** and the chairperson makes sure that these rules are followed. This is the most senior official within the club. The chairperson would represent the club at any other meetings.

The Royal and Ancient Golf Club – The headquarters of golf

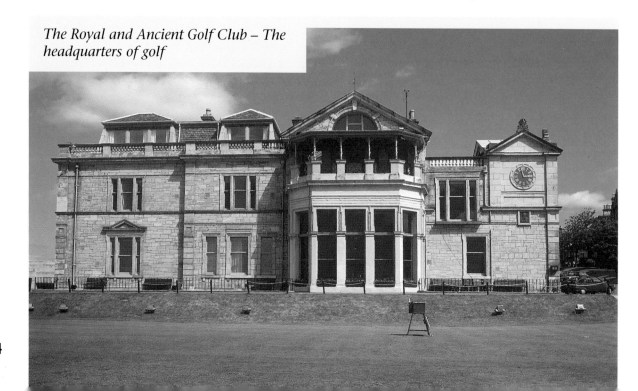

Officials of a small club discussing club business

- The **vice-chairperson** (VC) deputizes for the chairperson if they are unable to do their job for some reason. The VC may need to run meetings and often needs to be available at short notice. If the chairperson is very busy, the VC will help by carrying out some of the duties.

- The **secretary** does a very important job in any club, and has to deal with most of the written work. The secretary may have to answer and write letters and keep the **minutes** (the record of what went on) of all of the meetings. This is usually one of the busiest and most demanding jobs, especially in a big club. If a club can afford to pay any of their officials, it is usually the secretary who is paid, as the job is so demanding.

- The **treasurer** deals with all the financial affairs of the club. This person would probably have to run a bank account on behalf of the club. This account is used to pay bills, bank the **subscriptions** taken and ensure that the club has enough money to pay for equipment or hire of facilities.

- Committee members are people who are elected by the members to manage the club. They have regular meetings where they take decisions on behalf of the club and ensure that it runs smoothly. There are often quite a lot of sub-committees within a club for such areas as team selection, fund-raising or even discipline.

- **Members** are all the people who join the club. You cannot hold any of the other positions within the club unless you are a member. You usually pay a fee or subscription to belong to the club. The members usually have the right to have a say in how the club should be run. They are all entitled to go to the Annual General Meeting (AGM), where all of the officials of the club are elected for the forthcoming year.

5

Open days can encourage new people to try out a sport

What clubs do

All the clubs that exist, at any of the different levels, perform their own particular functions:

- *Providing facilities* – a sports club must have somewhere where the members can play their sport. Sometimes, if it is a big club, it may own its own facilities – as would be the case with a golf club. Many smaller clubs hire or rent the facilities where they play. These clubs need to decide when and how the facilities could be used, and there is usually some kind of booking system which they would manage.

- *Organization of competitions and events* – this is one of the main functions of a sports club, and a variety of different types of competition would be included. The club is likely to be involved in playing competitively against other clubs and at different levels. However, the clubs also have to cater for those members who just want to play for fun or for their own personal pleasure and who do not particularly want to compete.

- *Promotion of their sport* – this can take many forms. The club will need to promote its particular sport, so that it can continue to attract members. The clubs may have **open days**, where anyone is invited to come along and join in. They may also have **taster sessions**, where people are given some basic instruction in the sport and offered an opportunity to try it out.

- *Encouragement for juniors* – many clubs have a junior or youth section which caters specifically for young players. Every club needs to get young players involved, to ensure that it will keep going and prosper in the future. Some clubs may even adapt their particular sport to suit young players; short tennis played at tennis clubs is a good example of this.

- *Community status and involvement –* all clubs, from large professional ones through to small local ones, can help by being involved in the local community. By getting people involved in trying out or taking part in sport, they may attract them as supporters or spectators, and this may lead to new members joining. Many professional soccer clubs attract tens of thousands of supporters to their games. This encourages a large part of the community to be united behind the club.

Professional clubs

These clubs are run as businesses and they are usually privately owned. This means that they are not run in the same way as small, local sports clubs. They may well have the same types of officials, but these will be employed full-time and will be paid for their services. The players, or people who take part in the sport, will also be full-time, paid professionals who make their living out of playing their sport.

Local authorities

All local authorities, such as local and regional councils, have a duty to make provision for sport in their area. This means that they may provide coaching courses as well as the basic facilities for people to play and take part in the sport. They usually do this through:

- school and educational facilities

- leisure centres.

All schools must have some sports facilities, so that Physical Education (PE) can be taught. It is one of the subjects that, by law, *must* be taught within a school. This often results in there being an arrangement for **dual use** or **dual provision (joint provision)** so that these facilities can be used by others:

- **dual use** means that the school has the use of the facilities during the day and at other times they are available for public use.

- **dual provision** means that the facilities are jointly used and owned; the public and the school may even be sharing them at the same time.

Anyone can use facilities with dual use and dual provision

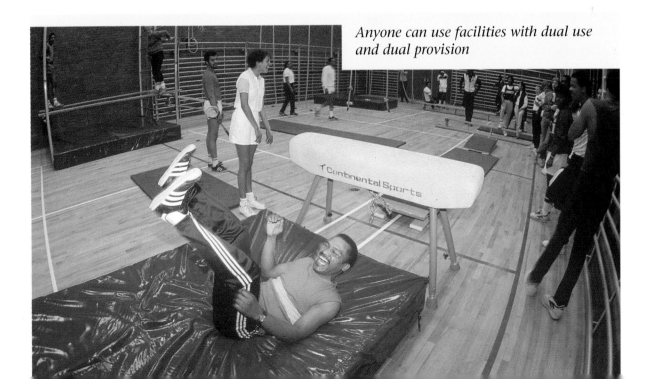

Most schools arrange inter school matches and fixtures

School organization

For the majority of young people, school is the main place where they play sports. This is because sport is compulsory, so every pupil takes part. In addition, many schools provide **extra-curricular activities**, which take place outside of the normal time-tabled lessons. These usually include extra sporting activities. They may take place during the lunch-time breaks or, more commonly, after school has finished in the afternoons. Some are even held during the weekends.

Some schools have built up the tradition for holding regular sporting fixtures, for example on Wednesday afternoons and on Saturday mornings. This can lead to many ex-pupils continuing to play sport together. They may even form teams and compete as 'former pupils'.

However, not all schools can provide a full range of extra-curricular activities, so it is important that they establish links with other organizations that can.

Sporting links

Clubs are very keen to encourage young people to join. One of the best ways for clubs to get young people interested in sport – and to keep them interested – is by forming strong links with schools. A club may be able to provide extra coaching in activities which the school already offers. Alternatively, the club could give opportunities in a completely different activity, which the school is unable to offer because it lacks the facilities, staff expertise, time or specialist equipment. A strong link between clubs and schools benefits both because:

- the clubs will be keen to keep their standards up;

- the schools' pupils are able to have extra practice and training.

Many professional clubs (especially soccer clubs) even send **scouts** to the schools to watch matches and invite the young players to join them. These scouts are members of the club staff whose job it is to find, and sign on, talented youngsters.

If the clubs can get talented players to join them when they are quite young, they don't need to spend vast amounts of money buying players from other clubs in the future. This is why many clubs have youth policies and run several youth teams made up of local young players.

Encouraging young people to continue to take an active part in sport has been a priority for many years. Research that was carried out showed that young people quickly lose interest in sport when they leave school and stop taking part in it. This was known as the **Wolfendon Gap** (named after the writer of a report).

Not all young people actively take part in sport

This is why the clubs have been encouraged to set up strong links with schools, to ensure that more young people continue to take part. The increase in the amount of facilities now available has also greatly improved the situation. There was a time when young people could not continue with an activity – even if they wanted to – because the only facilities were in the schools and they could not use them once they had left.

The role of national governing bodies

Each of the various sports is run by its own national governing body. Although these bodies do not actually manage their sport at all levels, they do make the rules and issue the guidelines which all of the regional and local organizations have to follow. They decide on:

- finance
- fixtures
- discipline
- coaching
- promotion and advertising.

The majority of people who help with the organization of sport do so as volunteers. In the governing bodies, there are paid officials in the most responsible jobs.

Fact File

There are over 200 governing bodies of sport in the UK alone. Just about every sport you could think of has one!

2 Competitions

Most sport is competitive. For many people this is an important reason why they like to play it. However, the type of competition has to be carefully selected and it must be well organized. Competitions may take the form of:

- knockouts
- leagues
- round robins
- ladders.

Clubs may use any or all of the above, because the organizers must try to find the fairest possible way to run their competitions.

Knockouts

These competitions are very popular. They are often used when there is a very large number of people or teams taking part, because it is the quickest and easiest type of competition to organize.

The event is always played in **rounds**. This means that each team plays against one other team and the winner then goes through to the next round. The number of teams taking part is halved in each round, as the losing teams drop out. This is the main disadvantage of this type of competition: teams only get one chance to compete. The second best team in the entire competition could get knocked out in the very first round and a less skilful team could get to the final!

To avoid this, many competitions have **seeded** teams or players. The organizers spread out the best players or teams throughout the draw for the competition,

so that the two top ones can only meet if they both get through to the final. The Wimbledon tennis championship is organized along these lines. However, it does depend upon the organizers taking the right decisions about who the best players are! They can be helped to do this by computer programs that keep a constant and updated record of all of the players' performances, and then gives them a **ranking position**.

Wimbledon , a knockout competition

Another way of organizing a competition is to have preliminary rounds, where less skilful teams play against each other for the right to play against the top teams or players in the later rounds. This method is often used in soccer competitions, because the game is very popular and large numbers of teams and players want to take part. It happens in the soccer World Cup (which is played in qualifying groups) and also in the Football Association Cup (the FA Cup). Most of the international competitions in any sport start with a qualifying stage and end with a knockout stage.

Fact File

When the final stages of one year's FA Cup are taking place, some teams are already involved in the preliminary stages for the right to play in the next year's!

Organizing a knockout competition can be very complicated because you need rounds with possibly 128, 64, 32, 16, 8, 4 and finally 2 players or teams. You must always 'knock out' half the teams or players, in every round. You may not always have the right number of entries for this system but the competition will not work any other way! The solution to the problem of having too few entries is to have a preliminary round with **byes** (some of the teams or players do not take part). Then you end up with the right numbers for your proper first round.

So that teams or players can have further opportunities to play when they have been knocked out in the first round, some

knockout competitions organize a **plate competition**. All of the first round losers take part in another knockout competition, which is again played up to a final. This at least guarantees all of the players at least two games and keeps up interest in the competition.

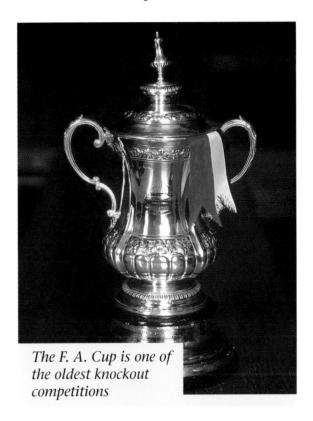

The F. A. Cup is one of the oldest knockout competitions

Fact File

In most sports, at least one knockout competition is organized because the format is very exciting and it generates a lot of interest from supporters and fans. It is very rare for any team to win both the knockout competition and league competition of their sport. To win both is known as 'the double'.

Leagues

This is a very common and popular type of competition and it is often considered to be one of the hardest to win, and therefore the most important. A league usually has to take place over a long period of time. It rewards the most consistent team or player, who as a result manages to finish up at the top of the league.

Most sports have a particular **season** when they are played. The league competition will run throughout this season. A league competition is well-suited to include a large number of teams, or entries, as it gives them all a chance to play and also makes sure that they have a lot of games. Each team plays against each of the others at least once. Often they play twice, once at home and once away. The teams get points for winning or drawing games or matches. They do not usually get any points at all if they lose a match!

Because there may be a large number of teams wishing to take part in one particular sport, the leagues may be split up into divisions. Opposite is an example of the different divisions of professional soccer in England.

English football leagues

Professional soccer in England is the largest organized league in the country, with a total of 92 professional teams included in all of the divisions. Each season they all play against each other. The teams in the Premier League try to finish top of their league, to win the League Championship and be the top team in the country.

The teams at the bottom of the Premier League also have to try to avoid being **relegated** to a lower division. Within the other leagues there are many teams trying to be **promoted** to the higher divisions, and many trying not to be relegated to the lower divisions. The very bottom team of the lowest league (the third division) actually has to drop out of the Football League altogether and is replaced by the top team from the **GM Vauxhall Conference** (this league is named after the sponsors, so it is likely to change!). There is a whole set of other leagues below the Football League, and they also have their own promotion and relegation arrangements.

Many players start their careers in these lower leagues, where a lot of the players are **semi-professional** (they have jobs as well as getting paid for playing soccer). They try to work their way up through the system until they end up playing for one of the top professional clubs. This system can also work in reverse. As players grow older, they often drop down divisions and may play at lower levels towards the end of their careers.

Some of the many advantages to organizing activities on a league basis are that:

- fixtures can be arranged in advance and publicized;

- a certain number of games are guaranteed to be played;

- tickets (and season tickets) can be sold a long time in advance;

- it is the most profitable system over a long period of time, in terms of finance.

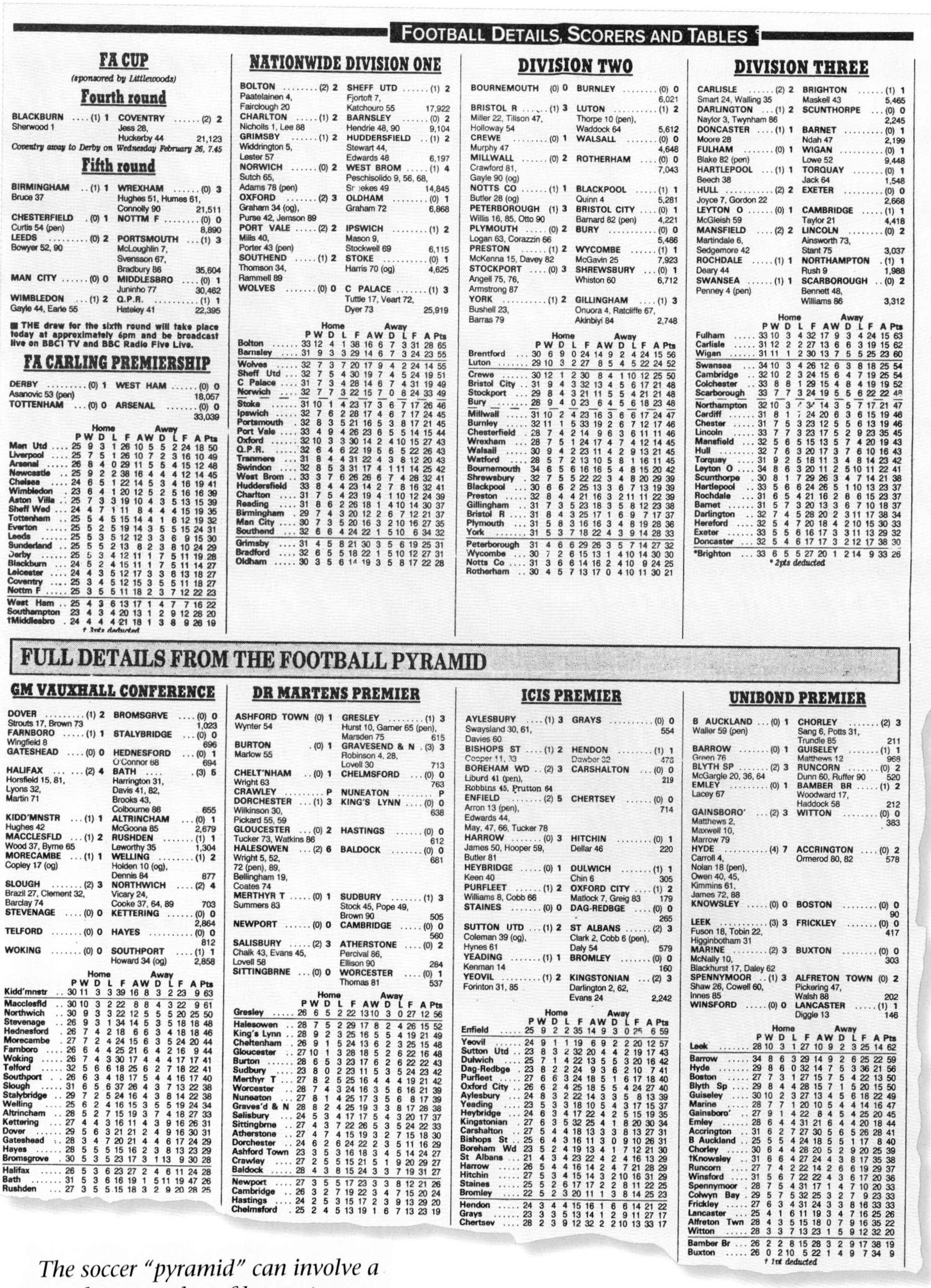

FOOTBALL DETAILS, SCORERS AND TABLES

FA CUP

(sponsored by Littlewoods)

Fourth round

BLACKBURN Sherwood 1	(1) 1	COVENTRY Jess 28, Huckerby 44	(2) 2	21,123

Coventry away to Derby on Wednesday February 26, 7.45

Fifth round

BIRMINGHAM Bruce 37	(1) 1	WREXHAM Hughes 51, Humes 61, Connolly 90	(0) 3	21,511
CHESTERFIELD Curtis 54 (pen)	(0) 1	NOTTM F	(0) 0	8,890
LEEDS Bowyer 52, 90	(0) 2	PORTSMOUTH McLoughlin 7, Svensson 67, Bradbury 86	(1) 3	35,604
MAN CITY	(0) 0	MIDDLESBRO Juninho 77	(0) 1	30,462
WIMBLEDON Gayle 44, Earle 55	(1) 2	Q.P.R. Hateley 41	(1) 1	22,395

■ THE draw for the sixth round will take place today at approximately 6pm and be broadcast live on BBC1 TV and BBC Radio Five Live.

FA CARLING PREMIERSHIP

DERBY Asanovic 53 (pen)	(0) 1	WEST HAM	(0) 0	18,057
TOTTENHAM	(0) 0	ARSENAL	(0) 0	33,039

	Home						Away					
	P	W	D	L	F	A	W	D	L	F	A	Pts
Man Utd	25	9	3	1	26	10	5	5	2	24	18	50
Liverpool	25	7	5	1	26	10	7	2	3	16	10	49
Arsenal	26	8	4	0	29	11	5	5	4	15	12	48
Newcastle	25	9	2	2	38	16	4	4	4	12	14	45
Chelsea	24	6	5	1	22	14	5	3	4	16	19	41
Wimbledon	23	6	4	1	20	12	5	2	5	16	16	39
Aston Villa	25	7	3	3	19	10	4	3	5	13	15	39
Sheff Wed	24	4	7	1	11	8	4	4	4	15	19	35
Tottenham	25	5	4	5	15	14	4	1	6	12	19	32
Everton	25	5	2	5	19	14	3	5	5	15	24	31
Leeds	25	5	3	5	12	12	3	3	6	9	15	30
Sunderland	25	5	5	2	13	8	2	3	8	10	24	29
Derby	25	5	3	4	12	11	1	7	5	11	19	28
Blackburn	24	5	2	4	15	11	1	7	5	11	14	27
Leicester	24	4	3	5	12	17	3	3	6	13	18	27
Coventry	25	3	4	5	12	15	3	5	5	11	18	27
Nottm F	25	3	5	5	11	18	2	3	7	12	22	23
West Ham	25	4	3	6	13	17	1	4	7	7	16	22
Southampton	23	4	3	4	20	13	1	2	9	12	28	20
†Middlesbro	24	4	4	4	21	18	1	3	8	9	26	19

† 3pts deducted

NATIONWIDE DIVISION ONE

BOLTON Paatelainen 4, Fairclough 20	(2) 2	SHEFF UTD Fjortoft 7, Katchouro 55	(1) 2	17,922
CHARLTON Nicholls 1, Lee 88	(1) 2	BARNSLEY Hendrie 48, 90	(0) 2	9,104
GRIMSBY Widdrington 5, Lester 57	(1) 2	HUDDERSFIELD Stewart 44, Edwards 48	(1) 2	6,197
NORWICH Sutch 65, Adams 78 (pen)	(0) 2	WEST BROM Peschisolido 9, 56, 68, Sneekes 49	(1) 4	14,845
OXFORD Graham 34 (og), Purse 42, Jemson 89	(2) 3	OLDHAM Graham 72	(0) 1	6,868
PORT VALE Mills 40, Porter 43 (pen)	(2) 2	IPSWICH Mason 9, Stockwell 69	(1) 2	6,115
SOUTHEND Thomson 34, Rammell 89	(1) 2	STOKE Harris 70 (og)	(0) 1	4,625
WOLVES	(0) 0	C PALACE Tuttle 17, Veart 72, Dyer 73	(1) 3	25,919

	Home						Away					
	P	W	D	L	F	A	W	D	L	F	A	Pts
Bolton	33	12	4	1	38	16	6	7	3	31	28	65
Barnsley	31	9	3	3	29	14	6	7	3	24	23	55
Wolves	32	7	3	7	20	17	9	4	2	24	14	55
Sheff Utd	32	7	5	4	30	19	7	4	5	24	19	51
C Palace	31	7	3	4	28	14	6	7	4	31	19	49
Norwich	32	7	7	3	22	15	7	0	8	24	33	49
Stoke	31	10	1	4	23	17	3	6	7	17	26	46
Ipswich	32	7	6	2	28	17	4	6	7	17	24	45
Portsmouth	32	8	3	5	21	16	5	3	8	17	21	45
Port Vale	33	4	9	4	26	23	6	5	5	14	15	44
Oxford	32	10	3	3	30	14	2	4	10	15	27	43
Q.P.R.	32	6	4	6	22	19	5	6	5	22	26	43
Tranmere	31	8	4	4	31	22	4	3	8	12	20	43
Swindon	32	8	5	3	31	17	4	1	11	14	25	42
West Brom	33	3	7	6	26	26	6	7	4	28	32	41
Huddersfield	33	8	4	4	23	14	2	7	8	16	32	41
Charlton	31	7	5	4	23	19	4	1	10	12	24	39
Reading	31	8	6	2	26	18	1	4	10	14	30	37
Birmingham	29	7	4	3	20	12	2	6	7	12	21	37
Man City	30	7	3	5	20	16	3	2	10	16	27	35
Southend	32	6	6	4	24	22	1	5	10	6	34	32
Grimsby	31	4	5	8	21	30	3	5	6	19	25	31
Bradford	32	6	5	5	18	22	1	5	10	12	27	31
Oldham	30	3	5	6	14	19	3	5	8	17	22	28

DIVISION TWO

BOURNEMOUTH	(0) 0	BURNLEY	(0) 0	6,021
BRISTOL R Miller 22, Tillson 47, Holloway 54	(1) 3	LUTON Thorpe 10 (pen), Waddock 64	(1) 2	5,612
CREWE Murphy 47	(0) 1	WALSALL	(0) 0	4,648
MILLWALL Crawford 81, Gayle 90 (og)	(0) 2	ROTHERHAM	(0) 0	7,043
NOTTS CO Butler 28 (og)	(1) 1	BLACKPOOL Quinn 4	(1) 1	5,281
PETERBOROUGH Willis 16, 85, Otto 90	(1) 3	BRISTOL CITY Barnard 82 (pen)	(0) 1	4,221
PLYMOUTH Logan 63, Corazzin 66	(0) 2	BURY	(0) 0	5,486
PRESTON McKenna 15, Davey 82	(1) 2	WYCOMBE McGavin 25	(1) 1	7,923
STOCKPORT Angell 75, 76, Armstrong 87	(0) 3	SHREWSBURY Whiston 60	(0) 1	6,712
YORK Bushell 23, Barras 79	(1) 2	GILLINGHAM Onuora 4, Ratcliffe 67, Akinbiyi 84	(1) 3	2,748

	Home						Away					
	P	W	D	L	F	A	W	D	L	F	A	Pts
Brentford	30	6	9	0	24	14	9	2	4	24	15	56
Luton	29	10	3	2	27	8	5	4	5	22	24	52
Crewe	30	12	1	2	30	8	4	1	10	12	25	50
Bristol City	31	9	4	3	32	13	4	5	6	17	21	48
Stockport	29	8	4	3	21	11	5	5	4	21	21	48
Bury	28	9	4	0	23	6	4	5	6	18	23	48
Millwall	31	10	2	4	23	16	3	6	6	17	24	47
Burnley	32	11	1	5	33	19	2	6	7	12	17	46
Chesterfield	28	7	4	2	14	9	6	3	6	11	11	46
Wrexham	28	7	5	1	24	17	4	7	4	12	14	45
Walsall	30	9	4	2	23	11	4	2	9	13	21	45
Watford	28	5	7	2	13	10	5	8	1	16	11	45
Bournemouth	34	6	5	6	16	16	5	4	8	15	20	42
Shrewsbury	32	7	5	5	22	22	3	4	8	20	29	39
Blackpool	30	6	6	2	25	13	3	6	7	13	19	39
Preston	32	8	4	4	21	16	3	2	11	11	22	39
Gillingham	31	7	3	5	23	18	3	5	8	12	23	38
Bristol R	31	8	4	3	25	17	1	6	9	7	17	37
Plymouth	31	5	8	3	16	16	3	4	8	19	28	36
York	31	5	3	7	18	22	4	3	9	14	28	33
Peterborough	31	4	6	6	29	26	3	5	7	14	27	32
Wycombe	30	7	2	6	15	13	1	4	10	14	30	30
Notts Co	31	3	6	6	14	16	2	4	10	9	24	25
Rotherham	30	4	5	7	13	17	0	4	10	11	30	21

DIVISION THREE

CARLISLE Smart 24, Walling 35	(2) 2	BRIGHTON Maskell 43	(1) 1	5,465
DARLINGTON Naylor 3, Twynham 86	(1) 2	SCUNTHORPE	(0) 0	2,245
DONCASTER Moore 28	(1) 1	BARNET Ndah 47	(0) 1	2,199
FULHAM Blake 82 (pen)	(0) 1	WIGAN Lowe 52	(0) 1	9,448
HARTLEPOOL Beech 38	(1) 1	TORQUAY Jack 64	(0) 1	1,548
HULL Joyce 7, Gordon 22	(2) 2	EXETER	(0) 0	2,668
LEYTON O McGleish 59	(0) 1	CAMBRIDGE Taylor 21	(1) 1	4,418
MANSFIELD Martindale 6, Sedgemore 42	(2) 2	LINCOLN Ainsworth 73, Stant 75	(0) 2	3,037
ROCHDALE Deary 44	(1) 1	NORTHAMPTON Rush 9	(1) 1	1,988
SWANSEA Penney 4 (pen)	(1) 1	SCARBOROUGH Bennett 48, Williams 86	(0) 2	3,312

	Home						Away					
	P	W	D	L	F	A	W	D	L	F	A	Pts
Fulham	33	10	3	4	32	17	9	3	4	24	15	63
Carlisle	31	12	2	2	27	13	6	6	3	19	15	62
Wigan	31	11	1	2	30	13	7	5	5	25	23	60
Swansea	34	10	3	4	26	12	6	3	8	18	25	54
Cambridge	32	10	2	3	24	15	6	4	7	19	25	54
Colchester	33	8	8	1	29	15	4	8	4	19	19	52
Scarborough	33	7	7	3	24	19	5	5	6	22	22	48
Northampton	32	10	3	4	34	14	3	5	7	17	21	47
Cardiff	31	8	1	7	24	20	6	3	6	15	19	46
Chester	31	7	5	3	23	12	5	5	6	13	19	46
Lincoln	33	7	7	3	23	17	5	2	9	23	35	45
Mansfield	32	5	6	5	15	13	5	7	4	20	19	43
Hull	32	7	6	3	20	17	3	7	6	10	16	43
Torquay	31	9	2	5	18	11	3	4	8	14	23	42
Leyton O	34	8	6	3	20	11	2	5	10	11	22	41
Scunthorpe	30	8	1	7	29	26	3	4	7	14	21	38
Hartlepool	33	5	6	6	24	26	5	1	10	13	23	37
Rochdale	31	6	5	4	21	16	2	8	6	15	23	37
Barnet	31	5	7	3	20	13	3	6	7	10	18	37
Darlington	32	7	4	5	28	20	2	3	11	17	38	34
Hereford	32	5	4	7	20	18	4	2	10	15	30	33
Exeter	33	5	5	6	16	17	3	3	11	13	29	32
Doncaster	32	5	4	6	17	17	3	2	12	17	38	30
*Brighton	33	6	5	5	27	20	1	2	14	9	33	26

* 2pts deducted

FULL DETAILS FROM THE FOOTBALL PYRAMID

GM VAUXHALL CONFERENCE

DOVER Strouts 17, Brown 73	(1) 2	BROMSGRVE	(0) 0	1,023
FARNBORO Wingfield 8	(1) 1	STALYBRIDGE	(0) 0	696
GATESHEAD	(0) 0	HEDNESFORD O'Connor 68	(0) 1	694
HALIFAX Horsfield 15, 81, Lyons 32, Martin 71	(2) 4	BATH Harrington 31, Davis 41, 82, Brooks 43, Colbourne 86	(3) 5	655
KIDD'MNSTR Hughes 42	(1) 1	ALTRINCHAM McGoona 85	(0) 1	2,679
MACCLESFLD Wood 37, Byrne 65	(1) 2	RUSHDEN Leworthy 35	(1) 1	1,304
MORECAMBE Copley 17 (og)	(1) 1	WELLING Holden 10 (og), Dennis 84	(1) 2	877
SLOUGH Brazil 27, Clement 32, Barclay 74	(2) 3	NORTHWICH Vicary 24, Cooke 37, 64, 89	(2) 4	703
STEVENAGE	(0) 0	KETTERING	(0) 0	2,864
TELFORD	(0) 0	HAYES	(0) 0	812
WOKING	(0) 0	SOUTHPORT Howard 34 (og)	(1) 1	2,858

	Home						Away					
	P	W	D	L	F	A	W	D	L	F	A	Pts
Kidd'mnstr	30	11	3	3	39	16	8	3	2	23	9	63
Macclesfld	30	10	3	2	22	8	8	4	3	22	9	61
Northwich	30	9	3	3	22	12	5	5	5	20	25	50
Stevenage	26	9	3	1	34	14	5	3	5	18	18	48
Hednesford	26	7	4	2	18	6	6	3	4	18	18	46
Morecambe	27	7	2	4	24	15	6	3	5	24	20	44
Farnboro	26	6	4	4	25	21	6	4	2	16	9	44
Woking	26	7	4	3	30	17	4	4	4	17	17	41
Telford	32	5	6	6	18	25	6	2	7	18	22	41
Southport	26	6	3	4	18	17	5	4	4	16	17	40
Slough	31	6	5	6	37	26	4	3	7	13	22	38
Stalybridge	29	7	2	5	24	16	4	3	8	14	22	38
Welling	25	6	2	4	16	15	3	5	5	19	24	34
Altrincham	28	5	2	7	15	19	3	7	4	18	27	33
Kettering	27	4	4	3	16	11	4	3	9	16	26	31
Dover	29	5	6	3	21	21	2	4	9	16	30	31
Gateshead	28	3	4	7	20	21	4	4	6	17	24	29
Hayes	28	5	5	5	15	16	2	3	8	13	23	29
Bromsgrove	30	5	3	5	23	17	3	1	13	9	30	28
Halifax	26	5	3	6	23	27	2	4	6	11	24	28
Bath	31	5	3	6	16	19	1	5	11	19	47	26
Rushden	27	3	5	5	15	18	3	2	9	20	28	25

DR MARTENS PREMIER

ASHFORD TOWN Wynter 54	(0) 1	GRESLEY Hurst 10, Garner 65 (pen), Marsden 75	(1) 3	615
BURTON Marlow 55	(0) 1	GRAVESEND & N Robinson 4, 28, Lovell 30	(3) 3	713
CHELT'NHAM Wright 63	(0) 1	CHELMSFORD	(0) 0	763
CRAWLEY	P	NUNEATON	P	
DORCHESTER Wilkinson 30, Pickard 55, 59	(1) 3	KING'S LYNN	(0) 0	638
GLOUCESTER Tucker 73, Watkins 86	(0) 2	HASTINGS	(0) 0	612
HALESOWEN Wright 5, 52, 72 (pen), 89, Bellingham 19, Coates 74	(2) 6	BALDOCK	(0) 0	681
MERTHYR T Summers 83	(0) 1	SUDBURY Stock 45, Pope 49, Brown 90	(1) 3	505
NEWPORT	(0) 0	CAMBRIDGE	(0) 0	560
SALISBURY Chalk 43, Evans 45, Lovell 58	(2) 3	ATHERSTONE Percival 86, Ellison 90	(0) 2	284
SITTINGBRNE	(0) 0	WORCESTER Thomas 81	(0) 1	537

	Home						Away					
	P	W	D	L	F	A	W	D	L	F	A	Pts
Gresley	26	6	5	2	22	13	10	3	0	27	12	56
Halesowen	28	7	5	2	29	17	8	2	4	26	15	52
King's Lynn	28	9	2	3	25	16	5	5	4	19	21	49
Cheltenham	26	9	1	5	24	13	6	2	3	25	15	48
Gloucester	27	10	1	3	28	18	5	2	6	22	16	48
Burton	28	6	5	3	23	17	6	2	6	22	22	43
Sudbury	23	8	0	2	23	11	5	3	5	24	23	42
Merthyr T	27	8	2	5	25	16	4	4	4	19	21	42
Worcester	28	7	4	3	24	16	3	5	6	16	21	39
Nuneaton	27	8	1	4	25	17	3	5	6	8	17	39
Graves'd & N	28	8	2	4	25	19	3	3	8	17	28	38
Salisbury	24	5	3	4	17	17	5	4	3	20	17	37
Sittingbrne	27	4	3	7	22	26	5	3	5	24	22	33
Atherstone	27	4	7	4	15	19	3	2	7	15	18	30
Dorchester	24	6	2	6	24	22	2	3	5	11	16	29
Ashford Town	23	3	5	3	16	18	3	4	5	14	24	27
Crawley	27	2	5	5	15	21	5	1	9	20	29	27
Baldock	28	4	3	8	15	24	3	3	7	19	31	27
Newport	27	3	5	5	17	23	3	3	8	12	21	26
Cambridge	26	3	2	7	19	22	3	4	7	15	20	24
Hastings	24	2	5	3	15	17	2	3	9	13	29	20
Chelmsford	25	2	4	5	13	19	1	6	7	13	23	19

ICIS PREMIER

AYLESBURY Swaysland 30, 61, Davies 60	(1) 3	GRAYS	(0) 0	554
BISHOPS ST Cooper 11, 33	(1) 2	HENDON Dawber 32	(1) 1	478
BOREHAM WD Liburd 41 (pen), Robbins 45, Prutton 64	(2) 3	CARSHALTON	(0) 0	219
ENFIELD Arron 13 (pen), Edwards 44, May, 47, 66, Tucker 78	(2) 5	CHERTSEY	(0) 0	714
HARROW James 50, Hooper 59, Butler 81	(0) 3	HITCHIN Dellar 46	(0) 1	220
HEYBRIDGE Keen 40	(0) 1	DULWICH Chin 6	(1) 1	305
PURFLEET Williams 8, Cobb 66	(1) 2	OXFORD CITY Matlock 7, Greig 83	(1) 2	179
STAINES	(0) 0	DAG-REDBGE	(0) 0	265
SUTTON UTD Coleman 39 (og), Hynes 61	(1) 2	ST ALBANS Clark 2, Cobb 6 (pen), Daly 54	(2) 3	579
YEADING Kenman 14	(1) 1	BROMLEY	(0) 0	160
YEOVIL Forinton 31, 85	(1) 2	KINGSTONIAN Darlington 2, 62, Evans 24	(2) 3	2,242

	Home						Away					
	P	W	D	L	F	A	W	D	L	F	A	Pts
Enfield	25	9	2	2	35	14	9	3	0	25	6	59
Yeovil	24	9	1	1	19	6	9	2	2	20	12	57
Sutton Utd	23	8	3	2	32	20	4	4	2	19	17	43
Dulwich	25	7	1	4	22	13	5	5	3	20	16	42
Dag-Redbge	23	8	2	2	24	9	3	6	2	10	7	41
Purfleet	27	6	6	3	24	18	5	1	6	17	18	40
Oxford City	26	6	2	4	25	18	5	5	4	24	27	40
Aylesbury	24	8	3	2	22	14	3	3	5	8	13	39
Yeading	23	5	3	3	18	10	5	4	3	17	15	37
Heybridge	24	6	3	4	17	22	4	2	5	15	19	35
Kingstonian	27	6	3	5	32	25	4	1	8	20	30	34
Carshalton	27	5	4	4	18	13	3	3	8	13	27	31
Bishops St	25	6	4	3	16	11	3	0	9	10	26	31
Boreham Wd	23	5	2	4	19	13	4	1	7	12	21	30
St Albans	21	4	3	4	23	22	4	2	4	16	13	29
Harrow	26	5	4	4	16	14	2	4	7	21	28	29
Hitchin	27	5	3	4	15	14	3	2	10	16	31	29
Staines	25	5	2	6	17	17	2	2	8	11	22	25
Bromley	22	5	2	3	20	11	1	3	8	14	25	23
Hendon	24	3	4	4	15	16	1	6	6	14	21	22
Grays	23	3	3	5	13	14	1	2	9	11	27	17
Chertsey	28	2	3	9	12	32	2	2	10	13	33	17

UNIBOND PREMIER

B AUCKLAND Waller 59 (pen)	(0) 1	CHORLEY Sang 6, Potts 31, Trundle 85	(2) 3	211
BARROW Green 76	(0) 1	GUISELEY Matthews 12	(1) 1	968
BLYTH SP McGargle 20, 36, 64	(2) 3	RUNCORN Dunn 60, Ruffer 90	(0) 2	520
EMLEY Lacey 67	(0) 1	BAMBER BR Woodward 17, Haddock 58	(1) 2	212
GAINSBORO' Matthews 2, Maxwell 10, Marrow 79	(2) 3	WITTON	(0) 0	383
HYDE Carroll 4, Nolan 18 (pen), Owen 40, 45, Kimmins 61, James 72, 88	(4) 7	ACCRINGTON Ormerod 80, 82	(0) 2	578
KNOWSLEY	(0) 0	BOSTON	(0) 0	90
LEEK Fuson 18, Tobin 22, Higginbotham 31	(3) 3	FRICKLEY	(0) 0	417
MAR!NE McNally 10, Blackhurst 17, Daley 62	(2) 3	BUXTON	(0) 0	303
SPENNYMOOR Shaw 26, Cowell 60, Innes 85	(1) 3	ALFRETON TOWN Pickering 47, Walsh 88	(0) 2	202
WINSFORD	(0) 0	LANCASTER Diggle 13	(1) 1	146

	Home						Away					
	P	W	D	L	F	A	W	D	L	F	A	Pts
Leek	28	10	3	1	27	10	9	2	3	25	14	62
Barrow	34	8	6	3	29	14	9	2	6	25	22	59
Hyde	29	8	6	0	32	14	7	5	3	36	21	56
Boston	27	7	3	1	27	15	7	5	4	22	13	50
Blyth Sp	29	8	4	4	28	15	7	1	5	20	15	50
Guiseley	30	10	2	3	27	13	4	5	6	18	22	49
Marine	28	7	7	1	20	10	5	4	4	14	16	47
Gainsboro'	27	9	1	4	22	8	4	5	4	25	20	45
Emley	28	6	4	4	31	21	6	4	4	20	18	44
Accrington	31	6	2	7	27	30	5	6	5	26	28	41
B Auckland	25	5	5	4	24	18	5	5	1	17	8	40
Chorley	30	6	4	4	28	20	5	2	9	20	25	39
†Knowsley	31	6	6	4	27	24	4	3	8	17	35	38
Runcorn	27	7	4	2	22	14	2	6	6	19	29	37
Winsford	31	5	6	7	22	22	4	3	6	17	20	36
Spennymoor	28	7	5	4	31	17	1	4	7	10	20	33
Colwyn Bay	29	5	7	5	32	25	3	2	7	9	23	33
Frickley	27	6	3	4	31	24	3	3	8	16	33	33
Lancaster	25	4	1	6	11	19	3	4	7	16	25	26
Alfreton Twn	28	4	3	5	15	18	0	7	9	16	35	22
Witton	28	3	3	7	13	23	1	5	9	12	32	20
Bamber Br	26	2	2	8	15	28	3	2	9	17	38	19
Buxton	26	0	2	10	5	22	1	4	9	7	34	9

† 1pt deducted

The soccer "pyramid" can involve a very large number of league teams

Round robin

In this type of competition all of the teams, or competitors, play against each other and the most successful are the winners. One of the drawbacks to this type of competition is that it can only be organized for a fairly small number of teams or players, otherwise it would take far too long!

This method is often used for individual or pairs events, in sports such as tennis and squash. There is often some form of qualifying stage, and the round robin is played during the final stages. One example is in tennis, where the top few players throughout the season are selected to play in a round robin

tournament, almost as a form of final championship for the season. This type of tournament is very attractive to stage, because the organizers can guarantee to have all of the top players playing against each other at some time. Then the public can see all of their favourite **match-ups** between players of similar high standards.

One possible drawback to a straight round robin is that there may be no outright winner, if no one wins all of their games. For this reason, there is usually a **play-off** at the end between the top two teams or players.

Ladders

These are often thought to be more 'social' competitions, as they tend to be played in clubs where there is not so much at stake in winning or losing.

All of the players have their names listed on a long 'ladder' and the idea is to challenge people who are above you on the ladder to games, and then to take their place in that higher position if you win. There are usually rules about who you can challenge, depending on how much higher up the ladder they are than you. For example, the bottom player could not challenge the player at the very top. They would have to work their way up the ladder over quite a long period of time.

This system should end up with the best player at the club being at the top of the ladder. Then the other players would be trying to improve their position. One of the main drawbacks to this system is that it does not encourage new players to join in. This is because it may take them a very long time to work their way up to the top of the ladder.

Many squash clubs use the ladder system

Combined competitions

No one type of competition is perfect. Many sports organizations decide to use a combination of several types of competition when running a tournament. Whatever type is run, there will always be claims that it is unfair in one way or another, so a combination is often thought to be the best. The main aims of a competition should be to:

- have as many games as possible;

- give teams more than one chance to qualify or win;

- allow as many teams as possible to play against each other;

- allow the best team or player to win in the end.

Nearly all international sport competitions start off on a league basis, usually in regions. The soccer **World Cup** is a good example of this. There may even be competitions among groups of countries or in continents. The winners go on to the final stages. Teams or players who qualify may then play in leagues again, or even in round robin competitions, before getting to the final stages.

Whatever type of competition the organizers choose, there usually has to be a knockout stage as the ultimate final. This is because:

- there is more tension and excitement in **head-to-head** finals;

- leagues can be won and decided before all of the games are played, which **de-motivates** teams and players and leads to an anti-climax;

- these are far more attractive propositions to the **media** (television, press and radio);

- time restrictions may dictate that there has to be a particular winner at one particular time, so holding replays or re-staging events is not possible.

The soccer World Cup is one of the major international competitions

3 Officials

No sporting event can be run properly without **officials** to take responsibility in almost every area. In a top tennis tournament such as Wimbledon you would need up to twelve officials for each of the games which take place and there would be several of these going on at the same time!

The officials at Wimbledon would include the **umpire** and all of the **line judges** as well as the **net cord judge**. For some other sporting events you may need even more than that! At major athletic events you need officials for all of the field events and the track events, and many of them need specialist knowledge, to do their job properly.

At most activities the officials have very important roles, as they have to organize the competitors and maintain the smooth running of the event or tournament. Very few officials are paid to do their jobs. Many of them are volunteers and only claim their travelling expenses for attending the activity.

In professional sports there are more full-time paid officials at the highest levels. There are two main reasons for this:

- the standards and rewards are high and the players and supporters demand the highest standards from the officials;

- the sports events raise enough money to be able to pay the officials.

Some activities and events require a lot of specialist officials

In most **amateur** sports events, or activities played at lower levels, none of the officials are paid. There is simply not enough money available.

In most amateur sporting events, there will be the bare minimum of officials. It is quite common for team members to take on the role. For example, in many soccer matches the substitutes act as linesmen (or referee's assistants) and in cricket matches it is common practice for players to take turns to umpire. In many activities it is not easy to get officials at all and it can be very difficult to get fully **qualified** ones.

Qualifying as an official

It takes quite a long time to qualify as an official in any recognized sporting activity and it usually means going on a course, which has to be paid for. The training has to be recognized by the **governing body** of that sport, who will often arrange it as well. It can take quite a long time to work up through all of the different levels, as all officials are expected to be experienced at lower levels before they are allowed to take control of an activity at the highest level.

In many sports it is common for ex-players to become officials once their playing careers are over. This is often the case in first-class cricket, where ex-players become umpires using a lot of the knowledge they gained as players.

Being an official can often be rather a thankless task as it is almost impossible to please everyone. However, without these people being in charge it would be impossible for the events to take place.

The responsibilities of the officials can vary. Their main job is to take charge and control the activity.

There are two main types of officials. **Senior officials** include:

- referees
- judges
- umpires.

Minor officials include:

- linesmen
- referee's assistants
- timekeepers
- scorers.

All of the officials have to work together, doing their various jobs, to make sure the activity runs smoothly. Other responsibilities they can have include:

- interpreting the rules, laws or regulations of the activity;
- checking the equipment to be used;
- making sure the correct number of players are taking part;
- timing the activity.

Fact File

At professional soccer matches there is always a reserve official ready to take the place of any of the assigned match officials, if necessary. For example, if the referee is unable to carry on for some reason, then the most senior referee's assistant would take his place.

Responsibilities

Each separate activity has its own particular responsibilities. The qualities which an official must have do not really differ between activities. They can be summarized as follows:

- *A full and thorough knowledge of the rules or regulations of the activity* – as the officials cannot refer to a rule book during a game, they must be prepared for, and know how to deal with, any incidents that might occur. Some activities have very complicated rules and some have so many it is almost impossible to know them all. In golf, for example, there are even local rules which only apply to a particular golf course. When activities have a complicated system such as this, the official in charge may need assistance and rulings can take some time to be finalized.

- *A fair approach to the game* – which means that the official does not favour one of the teams or players but is **impartial**. To make sure of this many activities at the highest level have **neutral** officials who may even come from a different country.

- *Good physical condition* – which may be as simple as having good eyesight or enough speed and basic fitness to keep up with the game they are controlling. Some sports even make their officials take an annual fitness test and some have a maximum age for officials, which is really a retirement age. This obviously only refers to sports where the referee has to play an active part.

- *Being firm and decisive* – when they are in charge, officials may need to prevent any arguments starting. Their decision is usually final, so they must stick to it.

Officials often need to consult on some decisions

Coaches

Coaches play a very useful part in any sport. A coach is usually a specialist in one activity and is responsible for preparing a performer, or performers in:

- correcting and improving technique;

- acquisition of skill;

- achieving an optimum physical state;

- maintaining an optimum mental state.

Coaches only usually work with performers at higher levels as it is a very demanding task. Many work full-time and are paid. In many individual activities, such as international athletics, many of the top performers employ their own personal coach who works with them, and even travels with them, all of the time. A coach can assist a performer or a team with:

- *preparing performances* – including choosing tactics, formations, strategies, game plans and fitness levels;

- *analysing performances* – by giving plenty of feedback, both during and after a performance, to help players to find ways to improve;

- *motivation and encouragement* – before or during a performance, this can make the difference between a performer winning or losing;

- *reviewing performances* – by examining the last performance in great detail to look for ways in which improvements can be made and to suggest any changes which might be needed.

One of the most important jobs of the coach is to analyse performances. This analysis can include the performer's actions or even those of the opponents.

Each activity has its own equipment which can make coaching easier. For example, cricketers use cricket nets, trampolinists may use harnesses, rugby players use scrummage machines and tennis players can use an automatic ball feeder.

Coaches can help to improve a performance

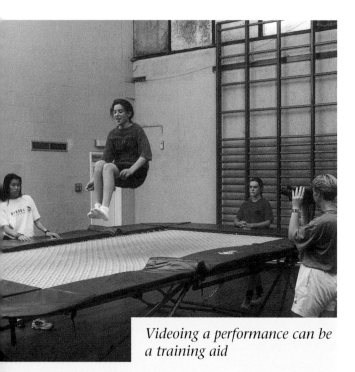
Videoing a performance can be a training aid

There are some common aids which can be used by coaches in all activities:

- *Video* – television or video film is now one of the coaches' most important aids. They can film other people's performances to show how something should be done. They can also film their own players to let them watch and analyse their own performance. Videos can be replayed in slow motion, which can show every little detail, as the movements can be filmed from a variety of angles. For example, a trampolinist who is **travelling** (moving forwards in the air when rotating) can benefit a great deal from watching it on video, because they can actually see how far they are travelling and correct it.

- *Demonstrations* – many coaches are ex-players or performers and they are therefore often able to demonstrate the right way to do something. If they cannot do this themselves, they can usually find someone else who can and

they can then point out the good features being shown. Sometimes they will take their team or players to watch a team of a higher standard, for the same reasons.

- *Books and coaching manuals* – coaches can recommend suitable books for performers to study. It is also very important for them to be able to keep up-to-date themselves. They may have to read a lot of articles in journals and keep up with current developments and any changes in rules.

- *Other specialists* – to prepare their performers fully, coaches may enlist the help of people such as:

  - **dieticians** (to work out the correct diet for the particular event);

  - **sports psychologists** (this is becoming a more important area as many coaches think that the only barriers left for the top performers at the top level are mental ones);

  - qualified **physiotherapists** (to deal with minor injuries, strains or pulls);

  - team doctors (to deal with emergencies).

- *Coaches' chalkboards* – these are small boards marked out with the playing area or pitch. The coach uses them during a game to point out positional changes or tactics.

Many advances have been made in recent years which can help to monitor, assist and even predict performances. Computer developments are among the most significant and many useful programs are now available.

Specialist computer programs can help select the most suitable training schedules for individual performers.

These performers can then be linked directly into the computers while they are training, to see what the effects are. In the 1996 Atlanta Olympic Games many of the competitors in the long-distance cycling events had specially-fitted chest monitors which recorded their heart rate and fed the information to a small read-out screen on their handlebars. This gave the cyclists an indication of just how hard their bodies were working and the limits to which they could push themselves.

Situations can be **simulated** by the computer so that the performer can virtually experience a game or competition and work out ways to play. Some Formula One racing drivers actually use very advanced computer games to simulate a race on a circuit which they have not driven before. This means they do not have to go to the circuit to become familiar with it.

More advanced equipment and training aids are being designed. These include the materials which are being used, such as lightweight clothing and lighter, safer equipment.

One of the most important aids for a coach is a very accurate timing device. These are now very advanced and can be specific to many activities. Being able to split times or lap times with a countdown facility is vital. Many conveniently-sized watches are now available that are designed for particular events.

Trainers

Trainers also play an important part in many sports. Their two main responsibilities are:

- *setting training schedules* – this can be over a long or short period of time and

Many long distance cyclists now wear monitors to check their heart rates

will be based on ensuring fitness levels and getting performers ready for competitions;

- *taking training sessions* – most clubs or individuals need someone to take on responsibility for this most basic of their provisions. The trainer makes sure that all the right things are included in each session, such as the warm-up. The main aim is to achieve the correct fitness level for every performer.

For high standards to be maintained in any sport, there must be some rules which say exactly how the activity should be played. Sometimes these rules are called laws or regulations.

All sports have rules covering:

- basic organization
- ease of administration
- safety
- enjoyment.

Most of the rules for the activities which are enjoyed today have developed over a long period of time. In the past, sporting activities did not have any set rules. However, as sports became more popular, and more widely played, it became necessary to set out basic guidelines, for the reasons listed above.

Basics

The playing area or surface to be used has to be defined and clearly stated. It is often important to standardize the length of time of the activity, the clothing to be worn, the equipment used and the number of people to take part.

Safety

One of the most important reasons for the introduction of rules is safety. Many of our present-day activities would be very dangerous if there were not very strict rules about foul play and the equipment to be used. Most of the rule changes which are made refer to making the activities safer.

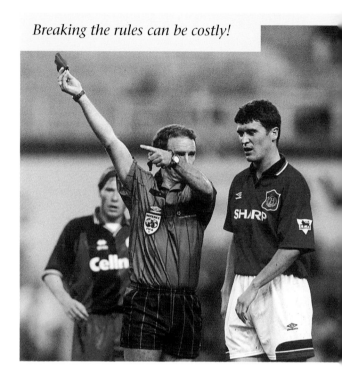

Breaking the rules can be costly!

Who makes the rules?

There are official bodies which set the rules for all of the activities which take place in this country. There are also international organizations which set the rules for sport throughout the world. In tennis, for example, the International Tennis Federation (ITF) has responsibility for the rules which apply throughout the world and they can over-rule decisions made by the Lawn Tennis Association, which sets the rules for the UK.

Many activities also have players' associations which work closely with the ruling bodies, setting and often – more importantly – enforcing the rules! These players' associations are more common in professional sport than they are in **amateur** sport.

Etiquette

Not all of the rules of an activity are actually written down; some of them are just 'accepted' by the people who take part. This is often known as **etiquette** and often takes the form of fair play, good manners or good sporting attitude.

In all activities there is accepted etiquette that it is not in the 'rule book'. It is up to the participants to behave in the right way. There is no real way to ensure that this does happen but players are very unpopular if they do not conform. This is another reason why there are players' associations. They will often take action against someone who is in breach of etiquette. Here are some examples of good etiquette:

- *Soccer* – if an opponent is injured, a player will kick the ball out of play to stop the match and allow the injured player to have treatment. On the re-start throw-in, the team will throw the ball back to their opponents who originally kicked the ball out of play.

- *Tennis* – at the end of a match, opponents shake hands and also thank and shake hands with the umpire.

- *Squash* – players will call their own foul shots such as 'double hit' and 'ball not up'.

Changes to rules

Rule changes can come about:

- to make the activity safer;

- to make the activity more exciting to attract more players or spectators;

- to keep up with the developments or changes in equipment or materials used.

Enforcement of rules

Rule enforcement is important and there is a system in all activities to make sure that it takes place. If a player does not abide by the rules, the actions that have to be taken can include:

- suspension

- a ban

- a fine

- expulsion from the sport.

All activities have penalties which can be applied when the game is in progress, such as the yellow and red card system in soccer, the **sin bin** in ice hockey and rugby league, and the fouled-out system in basketball. For more serious offences action will be taken after the event has ended. This can be for drug-taking, extreme foul play, illegal payments or 'bringing the game into disrepute' – doing something that may not be directly related to the sport, but which damages the 'image' of the sport.

Fact File

Many of the international bodies change or amend rules in competitions which they organize, so that they can try the new rules out. This was the case with many of the rule changes which were just experiments during the last soccer World Cup in America.

The Sports Council

This is an independent body which was set up in 1972 by a Royal Charter. It is responsible for sport as a whole in the UK but it also has separate councils for Scotland, Wales and Northern Ireland. It is probably the most important body in terms of the management of sport.

The members of the Council are all appointed by the Secretary of State for the Environment (a member of the Government) and it is a big organization with over 600 employees. The four aims of the Sports Council are to:

- increase participation in sport and physical recreation;

- improve the quality and quantity of sports facilities;

- raise standards of performance;

- provide information for and about sport.

The Sports Council helps and assists all types of sport

The Sports Council has identified specific ways that it tries to achieve these aims.

Increasing participation

Various surveys have been carried out to see how many people participate in sport. Only 10 per cent of women and 25 per cent of men take part in outdoor sport. For indoor sport, the figures are 18 per cent for women and 33 per cent for men. Nationally there are over 21.5 million adults and 7 million young people who participate in sport and physical recreation at least once a month. The Sports Council aims to increase this participation by:

- awarding regional participation grants to help local groups get people involved;

- running campaigns, such as 'Sport for All', 'Ever Thought of Sport?' and 'What's Your Sport?', to provide information and to encourage non-participants to take part;

- funding development staff to help the **governing bodies** for the different sports;

- organizing programmes to promote sport through other agencies.

Improving facilities

As well as trying to assist in the building of new facilities, the Council also tries to make better use of existing facilities. Its plan of action includes:

- encouraging provision of new and improved facilities by giving advice and some financial assistance;

A session arranged for young people to help raise standards of performance

- researching and preparing efficient and economical designs for sports buildings and systems;

- designing, building and testing innovative facilities and systems, including artificial playing surfaces and the use of computers;

- identifying good practice in design, facilities or management to be used elsewhere;

- funding research and feasibility studies into sports requirements.

Raising standards of performance

The Council has recognized that to achieve success at international level, the standards of sport at every level nationally must be improved. Because of the lack of success at many international sporting events, such as the 1996 Atlanta Olympics, the Council has been instructed to concentrate on raising performance standards. They are expected to use a great deal of their funds to do this. With this as their goal, the Council:

- runs five centres of excellence, at Crystal Palace, Bisham Abbey and Lilleshall (all of which are multi-purpose sports centres for swimming, tennis, gymnastics, athletics, football etc.), Plas y Brenin (mountain activities) and Holme Pierrepont (water sports);

- offers support to governing bodies, often financially, for excellence programmes, improving standards, coaching, international competition, facilities and equipment;

- finances the National Coaching Foundation to provide trained coaches;

- finds and encourages sponsors for top-class sport;

- finances and runs the campaign against drug abuse in sport, which involves taking responsibility for the drug-testing procedures and administration.

Not all sports have to be physically demanding!

Providing information

The Council is the main provider of information about sport. It achieves this:

- through a national information centre and nine regional offices;

- by briefing journalists, politicians, central and regional government, students and private organizations;

- by researching and providing data on all subjects to do with sport;

- by running conferences and exhibitions to do with sport.

How the Sports Council is financed

The Council receives a substantial government grant each year (in 1995–96 it was £47.5 million) and it also gets commercial sponsorship. It is involved in commercial activities such as publishing and endorsing merchandize, which brings in income. The efficient running of the national centres is also a source of income.

To help with the efficient running of the Council it has ten regional councils throughout the country. Their job is to bring together local people who are interested, including local authorities, voluntary organizations and the regional branches of governing bodies.

Central Council of Physical Recreation (CCPR)

This very important organization was founded in 1935. Its objectives are:

- to encourage as many people as possible (male and female) to participate in all forms of sport and physical recreation;

- to provide the separate governing bodies of the individual sports with a central organization to represent and promote their individual and collective interests.

These objectives are being met, as the CCPR now represents 209 UK sporting organizations, of which 68 are English. The membership varies from the National Federation of Anglers through to The Squash Rackets Association. All of the major governing bodies of popular sports are members and are represented.

The CCPR is a completely voluntary and independent organization. It has an executive committee which is elected from the members' governing bodies. There is a team of officers and secretarial staff who help to administer all of the policies and decisions which are made.

The CCPR and the Sports Council

The CCPR has very strong links with the Sports Council. There is not a direct connection, so that the CCPR keeps its independence, but it does act as an advisory body.

When the Sports Council was first set up in 1966 it was just an advisory body. It did not become properly established until 1972. At first, the CCPR encouraged sports groups to share both knowledge and experience. In 1971 the CCPR made over many of its assets to the Sports Council, including a number of national sports centres which it had established.

The governing bodies did not want to be part of the Sports Council and this is why the CCPR became a consultative body. However, the Sports Council does have clearly defined responsibility to the CCPR and this is the agreement which exists:

The Sports Council agrees that (so long as the CCPR is a body representing national organizations of sport and physical recreation as a whole) the Sports Council will make such resources and facilities available to the CCPR without cost to the CCPR as may be reasonably required.

So the CCPR has managed to make a very good arrangement with the Sports Council. It continues to maintain its independence but can still benefit greatly from all that the Sports Council can offer.

Because the membership of the CCPR is so large, it has grouped the governing bodies into six separate divisions:

- games and sports
- interested organizations
- major spectator sports
- movement and dance
- outdoor pursuits
- water recreation.

The growth of water recreation is a clearly defined area

Each of these divisions has the same administration structure and reports back to the main body.

The CCPR is a large body which costs a great deal of money to manage and operate. It has successfully raised funds through:

- donations from governing bodies;
- sponsorship from industry and commerce under the 'Sponsors of Sport' scheme;
- sponsorship by individuals or companies;
- sales and marketing of CCPR publications and research material;
- contracted financial support from the Sports Council.

In 1994 sponsors contributed £275 million and the advisory service of the CCPR raised more than £250,000 through commercial sponsorship. The services provided by the CCPR include:

- representing its members' interests – this can include media campaigns and formal and informal contact with other organizations;
- analysis of issues – such as developing women's sport, looking at competitive sports in schools, and sport and drugs;
- liaison with the Government – through both formal and informal contacts, which effectively work in both directions, schools have been offered advice on sport in the past;
- liaison with local authorities – as these are the greatest providers of facilities in the country this is a very important link;
- financial management and advice – this service, which the member bodies find very useful, includes the CCPR insurance scheme, adopted in the majority of schools, offering schoolchildren full protection against sporting injuries;

A community sports leaders award scheme course in action

- international contacts – for example, setting up festivals and conferences;

- information service – the CCPR produces a wide range of publications on a full range of activities.

Both **amateur** and **professional** sports have connections with the CCPR. One of the CCPR's major projects recently has been the Community Sports Leaders Award Scheme. Research showed that there are many volunteers who work in sport, so a scheme was set up to provide a basic award which is now provided at three levels.

So far there have been over 2500 courses and 35,000 leaders have qualified for:

- preliminary awards

- basic expedition training awards

- higher (Hanson) award.

Governing bodies

Each sport has to be separately organized and administered. The main responsibilities of the governing bodies who do this are:

- arranging local and national competitions;

- selecting teams for international competitions such as the Olympic Games and the various world championships;

- keeping players and participants in their particular sport informed;

- maintaining relationships with the media;

- drafting the rules and laws of the game (and making any changes and amendments);

- advancing the special interest of the sport.

They are also represented as members of the CCPR.

Individual help and coaching is a great benefit

Fact File

Over 50 million hours a year are given by volunteers who help out in sporting activities at all levels.

National Coaching Federation (NCF)

This was originally set up in 1983 by the Sports Council, to arrange coaching in all of the different sports. At that time it was based at Leeds Polytechnic but it is now nationwide, with different centres at colleges throughout the country.

The NCF is now a totally independent body with a committee made up of members from the Sports Council, the CCPR, the BOA and various other interested sports bodies. Although formed comparatively recently, the NCF has increased in importance very quickly over a short period of time, as the need for high quality and well-organized coaching has been recognized.

The National Trust

The National Trust was first formed in 1895 and it was given legal status in 1907 after the National Trust Act. This gave the Trust the right to designate its land 'inalienable'. This means that property and land that it owns cannot be sold or mortgaged; it will always be the property of the National Trust.

The Trust is a charity and it is the largest landowner and conservation society in Britain. Throughout the country it owns more than 230,000 hectares of land, with over 56,000 hectares of fell, dale, lake and forest in the Lake District alone. Access to land and property of the Trust is available to members, who pay an annual fee. However, much of the open land, moorland and coastal stretches are looked after and maintained by the Trust, and is freely accessible to everyone.

Walkers in the Lake District making full use of the countryside

Many walkers and people who enjoy the pleasures of outdoor activities are very grateful for the work the National Trust does, because it maintains all of these areas and keeps them available for their leisure pursuits.

Fact File

There are over sixty different types of volunteer helpers in the National Trust, ranging from pilots and surveyors to gamekeepers and calligraphers.

Dance performances can even be staged in the water

Countryside Commission

Created under the Countryside Act in 1968, the Countryside Commission replaced the National Parks Commission. It established over 160 country parks which are open and available to the public, giving anyone who enjoys the countryside and outdoor pursuits activities access to areas they can enjoy. Activities such as orienteering, mountain-biking and horse riding would be very restricted if these areas were not available. One very important advantage is that access is free and it is open to all.

The Arts Council

The Arts Council was established in 1946. In 1992 it was replaced by three new bodies: the Arts Council of England, The Scottish Arts Council and the Arts Council of Wales. There is also an Arts Council for Northern Ireland. These are the main funding bodies for the arts in their respective areas and are therefore very important to certain areas of sporting activity, such as dance.

The councils have a responsibility for developing and improving the knowledge and understanding of the arts. They are also responsible for increasing the accessibility of the arts to the general public. Their particular responsibility for dance is one of the most important areas in which they work. There is a requirement that dance is taught in schools so organizational links with the Arts Council have become vital.

The Arts Councils receive money from central government. They have also benefited greatly from funds from the **National lottery**, which have enabled them to carry out their responsibilities more widely. Dance is just one area of the performing arts where they assist, and even individuals are able to benefit from some help with funding.

Youth organizations

Many youth organizations provide sporting and leisure activities especially for young people. They mainly fall into two categories:

- youth clubs and organizations such as the National Association of Boys Clubs;

- uniformed organizations such as the Guides, the Scouts and the Air Training Corps.

These groups often promote outdoor pursuits, providing training and expertise. Many of them run their own award schemes which provide a very good basic knowledge. They also have access to (or own) facilities which are used for various leisure activities, and frequently run competitions. The National Association of Boys Clubs, for example, runs many boxing tournaments.

International Olympic Committee (IOC)

This is the governing body of the Olympic Games. Its main functions include:

- selecting host cities for the summer and winter games;

- approving the sports to be included in the Olympics;

Being chosen as an Olympic host city is a great achievement

- working with the host city, international governing bodies and international sports federations to plan the games.

New members of the IOC are elected by the current members. Representatives may be elected from any nation that has a national Olympic committee. Usually, each nation only has one representative, but nations which have hosted the games may have two.

Members used to be elected for life, but any member elected since 1965 must now retire at the age of 76. There is an executive board which handles many decisions and this is led by a president (who serves for eight years, but can then be re-elected for four-year terms), three vice-presidents and seven members (all these serve for four years).

Membership of the IOC brings with it a lot of power. Places are very sought-after, because the committee has such an influence on where the games are to be held. Just bidding to host the games has become a very complicated and expensive business. The committee members are invited to travel all round the world to assess the cities that would like to stage the games. There has often been controversy over their choice and there have even been claims that some of the members have been bribed with gifts, to get them to vote for one particular venue!

British Olympic Association (BOA)

This body works closely with the IOC. It promotes and manages all the British involvement with the Olympics. Its main responsibilities are organizing and choosing teams for the games and raising money to send them there.

The Olympic charter does not allow any political involvement, so the BOA is constantly involved in fund-raising. This always becomes more urgent as an Olympic year approaches.

The high status of the games means that sponsorship of the team is an attractive proposition for commercial bodies.

Fact File

The BOA always appears to become more active in the period just before an Olympic Games, as it tries to raise all of the money needed to send the British team to the games.

6 International sport

The remains of the Colosseum in Rome

The Olympic Games

The earliest recorded Olympic Games took place in 776 BC, in the stadium of Olympia, in ancient Greece, from where the Olympics get their name. They were held in honour of the God Zeus. Even that long ago, the stadium in which the games took place was quite impressive, as there was enough room for 40,000 spectators.

The Games were held every four years. All hostilities between the warring Greek states were stopped while the Games took place. Typical events at that time were wrestling, boxing, running (the main event was over 200 metres), discus, javelin, long jump and chariot racing. It is interesting to note that nearly all of those events still take place today.

The Games carried on in this way for many years until the reign of Emperor Theodosius in AD 394. He stopped them because he believed that the Games had lost their religious meaning and that the performers only took part for the riches of winning. It would be interesting to find out what he would think of the Olympics as they exist today!

The Olympics were not held again for 1500 years. Then, in 1896, they were re-launched in Athens, Greece. The links with the original Olympics went further than simply holding them in the same country. Many traditions were established, based on the old Games. Before the start of each Olympic Games, a torch is lit at Olympia using the sun's rays. This torch is carried by a relay of runners to the next **host city**'s stadium, and used to light a flame which then burns throughout the Games. However, modern technology does play its part because the flame is then usually kept alight by a gas supply during the two weeks of the Games!

The modern Olympics

The Olympic Games which have taken place since 1896 are referred to as the modern Olympics. They were re-started mainly through the efforts and determination of one man.

Baron Pierre de Coubertin was a French educationalist who had been very impressed by the way that sport was organized in England. He had made several visits and liked the way that events such as the Henley Regatta were run. This, together with the fact that in 1875 some German archaeologists had discovered the ruins of the original stadium in Olympia, made him decide to start up a movement to re-introduce the Games. In 1894 the International Olympic Committee was formed and it set about the task of organizing the games for 1896.

Baron de Coubertin believed that the Olympic movement which he had founded would promote world peace and harmony.

One of de Coubertin's famous quotes is displayed on the scoreboard at the opening of each games, as it is what he based his ideas on. It is also often kept on display during the Games:

The most important thing in the Olympic Games is not to win but to take part. Just as the most important thing in life is not the triumph but the struggle.

The **International Olympic Committee (IOC)** originally consisted of people chosen by de Coubertin himself, but it is now a very large body with representatives from all of the participating nations. This committee decides where the games are to be held. It was de Coubertin who decided that the Games should move all around the world and be awarded to a city rather than to a country. Now, cities have to make a bid to stage the Olympic Games and the final decision is made six years in advance, to give the host city enough time to prepare and get all of the facilities ready. At one time, not many cities were prepared to host the Games because they were very expensive and usually ran at a loss. This situation really changed after the 1984 Olympic Games in Los Angeles, USA, where the marketing and sponsorship of the Games resulted in a **surplus** being made.

Fact File

- *At the first modern Olympics of 1896, thirteen nations entered and the total number of athletes was 285. All of these were men because no women were allowed to enter!*

- *The Olympic closing ceremony always finishes with the releasing of doves to symbolize the peaceful spirit of the Games.*

In theory, the Games should not run at a profit, which is why they used the word 'surplus'. Once cities – and countries – realized that there was an opportunity to promote themselves, improve facilities and standards and make money as well, the whole business of bidding for and staging the Games took on more importance.

Now, there is nearly as much fuss and expense involved in making a bid to be the host as there is in actually staging the Games themselves.

The table below shows where the various summer and winter Olympic Games have taken place since they were re-introduced in 1896.

Year	Summer	Winter
1896	Athens, Greece	Not held
1900	Paris, France	Not held
1904	St Louis, USA	Not held
1908	London, England	Not held
1912	Stockholm, Sweden	Not held
1916	*World War I – no games held*	
1920	Antwerp, Belgium	Not held
1924	Paris, France	Chamonix, France
1928	Amsterdam, Holland	St Moritz, Switzerland
1932	Los Angeles, USA	Lake Placid, USA
1936	Berlin, Germany	Garmisch, Germany
1940	*World War II – no games held*	
1944	*World War II – no games held*	
1948	London, England	St Moritz, Switzerland
1952	Helsinki, Finland	Oslo, Norway
1956	Melbourne, Australia	Cortina, Italy
1960	Rome, Italy	Squaw Valley, USA
1964	Tokyo, Japan	Innsbruck, Austria
1968	Mexico City	Grenoble, France
1972	Munich, Germany	Sapporo, Japan
1976	Montreal, Canada	Innsbruck, Austria
1980	Moscow, USSR	Lake Placid, USA
1984	Los Angeles, USA	Sarayevo, Yugoslavia
1988	Seoul, S. Korea	Calgary, Canada
1992	Barcelona, Spain	Albertville, France
1994		Lillehammer, Norway
1996	Atlanta, USA	

The Olympic Games were the first major international sporting event. They are still the most important and successful of all of the events that take place. However, things have not always run smoothly and nearly all of the recent Games have been affected by problems of one sort or another. The following is a brief description of the major events which have affected recent games.

Berlin, 1936

The decision to award these Games to Berlin was made in 1931, two years before Adolph Hitler and his Nazi party came to power in Germany.

One of Hitler's main beliefs was that there was a master race, known as the Aryans. Supposedly, these people were blond and fair-skinned and were true Germans. The Nazis despised the Jews. By the time of the Olympics the Nazis had started to persecute the Jews and introduce separate laws for them.

Hitler tried to use the Games to promote all these ideas, turning the games into a propaganda exercise. One of the main reasons he failed was the success of a black American athlete, Jesse Owens.

Jesse Owens won four gold medals in the track and field events, much to Hitler's obvious disapproval. The American team had only narrowly voted to attend the Games because of Hitler's well-known views on black athletes and Jews. The success of the many black athletes in the American team was an embarrassment for Hitler and stopped him achieving what he had set out to do in terms of propaganda.

This was the most extreme case of political interference in any of the Olympic Games and it did make the organizers far more careful in selecting hosts.

Jesse Owens competing in Berlin in 1936

Fact File

ASPECTS OF P.E.

The Games organizers decided that from 1994 the Winter and Summer Olympics should be staggered, so some of the winter competitors would be able to take part in two Games in two years. This had never happened before.

Mexico City, 1968

One of the main **controversies** about these Games was that they had been awarded to Mexico City in the first place! This was because it is situated at a very high altitude and this helps the performance of athletes who usually train in these conditions. It also assists athletes in the shorter, more explosive events. There was genuine concern for performers in longer events, in case the **rarefied** atmosphere caused them breathing difficulties.

The cost of staging the event was also criticized. Mexico was a very poor country and a vast amount of money was spent just on staging the Games. The city of Tokyo, which had staged the Games four years earlier, had spent $200 million and it was doubtful if Mexico could really afford the money to pay for the Games.

Some black American athletes gave a 'Black Power' salute during the medal ceremony, by each raising a black-gloved fist. The first and third runners in the 200 metres, Tommie Smith and John Carlos, as well as the 440-metre relay team, were sent home for doing this. The athletes took this action to highlight the way that black people were treated in America. There was still a great deal of prejudice against black citizens in the United States at the time. The athletes chose this way to make their protest and make the world more aware of the problem.

One of the Palestinian terrorists with a member of the negotiating team during the hostage crisis in 1972

Munich, 1972

There was another Black Power protest by two Americans, Vince Matthews and Wayne Collett, during a medal ceremony when they failed to stand to attention. However, these Games were completely dominated by a terrorist attack on some of the athletes.

There was unrest in the Middle East and a group of Palestinian terrorists attacked members of the Israeli team. Eight terrorists attacked the Israeli quarters in the **Olympic village**. They killed two of the team and took nine others hostage. After a gun battle (seen throughout the world on television), all of the hostages, five terrorists and a German police officer were killed.

The security aspects of staging the Games were highlighted and were to become a major consideration for the Games in the future.

Montreal, 1976

South Africa had been banned from the Games since 1964 (Tokyo), because of the **apartheid** policy which existed in that country at that time. However, a rugby team from New Zealand had toured South Africa and so had upset most of the other African nations. The African nations threatened to **boycott** the Games unless the New Zealand team was banned.

New Zealand did take part and the African nations stayed away. Altogether a total of 30 nations did not go. This was to be the start of a long period of boycotts for various reasons.

The financial cost of these Games was also very high. Because of the incident in Munich the security had to be greatly increased. This was on top of the enormous cost of staging the Games. The city of Montreal continued to pay off the debt of staging the Games for many years.

Moscow, 1980

The choice of Moscow for these Games had been quite controversial because the Soviet Union had a poor record on human rights. However, they were one of the most successful competing countries in the history of the Olympics and had never hosted the Games before.

To make matters worse, the Soviet Union invaded the neighbouring country of Afghanistan in late 1979. It still had an invasion force there in 1980 at the start of the Games.

It was too late to change the venue for the Games but many countries demanded that the Soviet Union withdraw its forces or they would boycott the Games.

The Soviet Union refused to do this and many countries had to decide whether or not to send their competitors. Some countries, such as the USA, refused to send any. Great Britain advised its competitors not to go, but did not stop them if they wanted to. As a result of the boycott, a total of 52 nations, including the USA and Canada, did not attend. Many individuals also decided not to go.

Many thought that the Games were devalued because of this. The standard was inevitably lower with so many strong teams (such as the Americans) absent from the Games.

Part of the Olympic Games lavish opening ceremony

Los Angeles, 1984

As the venue was chosen six years in advance, the International Olympic Committee could not avoid America staging the Games immediately after it had boycotted those at Moscow in the Soviet Union. The two countries had not been very friendly anyway and there was a great fear that the Soviet Union would boycott the games as a way of retaliating against the USA. This is exactly what they did!

The Soviet Union, and fourteen other nations, boycotted the Games. The official reason they gave was concern over security arrangements. There was still ill-feeling between the USA and the Soviet Union over the invasion of Afghanistan and there were threats of demonstrations in America against the Soviet competitors.

There is little doubt that the worry about security was a convenient excuse for the Soviet Union to get its own back. Nearly all the other countries that boycotted were influenced by the Soviet Union, as they were also communist-ruled countries.

Another excuse was that the Games were being over-commercialized. The staging of the Games and its organization followed the American tradition of showmanship and the opening ceremony was one of the most spectacular ever seen. It set a precedent for other host cities to come up with similar very lavish ceremonies in future years. The whole of the event was sponsored by large, international companies and, for the first time, the Games ran at a large profit. This use of large-scale sponsorship was something which had come to stay and was used at later Games. However, all of this was against what the communist countries believed in.

Seoul, 1988

Seoul is in South Korea, which had a long-standing dispute with the neighbouring country of North Korea. There had been a war between the two countries in 1952 and the situation in 1988 was not much better. The IOC was greatly criticized for awarding Seoul the Games. There was much concern, right up until the start, that the facilities would not be ready and that the North Koreans would interfere. The North Koreans had already demanded that they be allowed to stage some of the events.

Weightlifter Andrew Davies, sent home from Barcelona for failing a drugs test

In the end there was very little disruption and the Games were quite successful. There was another boycott by five countries, including North Korea and Cuba. However, it is likely that more countries would have considered boycotting if the IOC had not introduced a rule that if countries did boycott the Games, all their officials would be excluded and not allowed to take part in decision-making. This clearly deterred many.

Sadly, the main controversy at these games involved positive drugs tests. Altogether, ten athletes were banned after testing positive for taking **performance-enhancing drugs**. The most famous was the Canadian sprinter, Ben Johnson. He had won the 100 metres in a world record time and was then stripped of his title two days later.

Fact File

In terms of the number of countries competing, Seoul was the most successful Games up until that time – 1988 – with 160 nations competing (compared to the 13 nations who took part in 1896).

Barcelona, 1992

After all the controversial events which had gone before, the 1992 Games were just about incident-free.

There was still some drug controversy as three British competitors – sprinter Jason Livingstone, and weightlifters Andrew Saxton and Andrew Davies – were tested positive and sent home.

A great deal of political change had occurred since the last Games. The Eastern European communist governments had collapsed and the Soviet Union had ceased to exist. This meant that there was no longer an East and a West German team but a single, unified German team. Also, all of the countries which had previously made up the Soviet Union now existed in their own right and were able to compete individually. There were twelve new competing countries from the former Soviet block and some individuals, who could not be considered to be from an affiliated nation, competed under the Olympic flag.

Another 'new' entry was South Africa, which was allowed to return to the Olympics for the first time since 1964. The South Africans had abolished the **apartheid** system. They entered a mixed-race team.

Fact File

The total number of sports was increased to 28 in 1992 with the addition of badminton and baseball, and the total number of medal events was increased by 20 to 257. There were over 12,000 athletes and officials involved in the Games.

Atlanta, 1996

The Games returned to the USA only twelve years after they had last been held there. This was slightly controversial in itself. The Games seemed to be going very smoothly, without any major incident except for some minor drug exclusions. However, there was a bomb explosion in one of the parks near to the Olympic athletic stadium, where there was entertainment for all the visitors and local people. Although the Games were not directly affected, the incident raised the whole issue of security again. It also affected the atmosphere and media coverage surrounding the events.

Another controversy involved the very high temperatures and high humidity which exists at this time of year in Atlanta. Special timings had to be introduced to allow some events to take place in the early hours of the morning. In all the equestrian events there were specially-constructed fans which sprayed water on to the riders and horses to prevent them from overheating. All the barriers which had separated **amateur** and **professional** sport were broken down by this time.

Many professional performers took part in their events in the Games. The most famous of these were the American basketball team and many of the leading tennis players from throughout the world.

Other international events

Commonwealth Games

The idea for staging some games for all the members of what had been the British Empire (countries previously governed and ruled by Great Britain) was first suggested in 1891. It was not until 1930 that the first such games took place. The venue was Hamilton in Ontario, Canada. At this time they were known as the British Empire Games. They have only been known as the Commonwealth Games since 1970.

There had been similar types of event before. Just after the 1920 Antwerp Olympics there was an athletics match between the USA and the British Empire, and the same thing happened after the 1924 Paris Olympics.

Atlanta's clsoing ceremony reminds the world of the venue for 2000

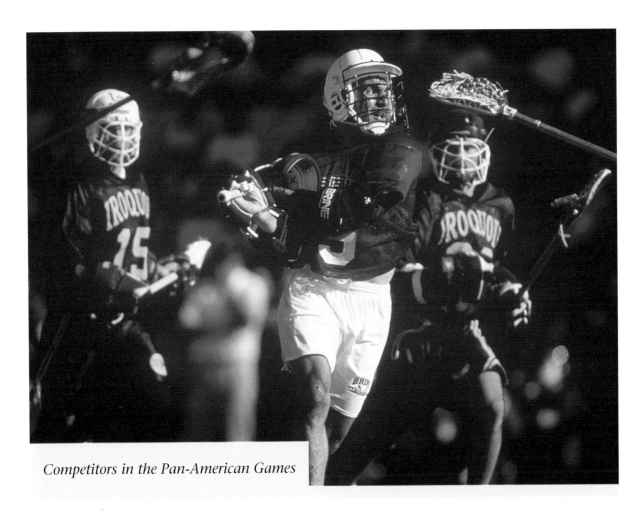

Competitors in the Pan-American Games

The Games follow the format of the Olympics very closely. They are also held every four years, following the Olympics by two years. They have a reputation for being the 'friendly games' and have not been as disrupted by boycotts or scandals as the Olympics.

Fact File

ASPECTS OF P.E.

In the first Commonwealth Games there were only eleven countries competing, whereas now there are 40. There were only six sports included, and women were only allowed to take part in the swimming events.

Pan-American Games

These Games were originally discussed in 1940 and should have started in 1942, but were delayed by World War II. They were started in 1951. The first Games were held in Buenos Aires.

The Pan-American Games now take place each year that falls immediately before an Olympic Games. They are open to any of the countries from North or South America and follow the Olympic format very closely, even down to a copy of the opening ceremony. The most recent Games took place in 1995 in Mar del Plata, Argentina.

Steffi Graff celebrates another Wimbledon championship

Wimbledon

The real name of the Wimbledon tennis tournament is the 'All England Tennis Championships', but it is open to players from any country. It is widely regarded as the most important tennis tournament of all. There is no official world championship in tennis, but many players regard the Wimbledon tennis tournament as one.

Originally Wimbledon was the home of the All England Croquet Club. The members decided to use the very well-prepared and tended lawns for tennis, as well. The first championships were held in 1877 and, apart from breaks for the World Wars, they have been held every year since.

In 1968 the organizers took the very bold step of declaring the championship to be an **open event** so that amateurs *and* professionals could play. This was the first major international competition to take this step and it paved the way for the breakdown of these barriers in other sports.

World championships

Many sports now stage their own world championships, and these are becoming established as major international sporting events. Some of them have begun only recently but it is unusual to find any major sport which does not have one.

Soccer

The world championship in soccer is usually known simply as the World Cup. This is because it was one of the very first world championships to be held in any of the major sports. The first World Cup took place in Uruguay in 1930. It had taken the ruling body of international soccer (FIFA)

Fact File

The large scale of the Wimbledon tournament can be seen by the money it generates. The 1994 championships made a record £28 million.

a long time to get it all organized. When the six member countries met in 1904 they decided to hold a tournament. The principle of the cup was not agreed until 1920 and the president of FIFA, **Jules Rimet** (after whom the first World Cup trophy was named), was influential in getting it under way. It remains one of the most popular and televized international events of all.

Cricket

Cricket was quite late in organizing a world championship. This was mainly due to the nature of the game. At test level, a game lasts for five days and a tournament on this basis would be just about impossible to arrange. The development of one-day knockout games meant that cricket could be played in a format that could be used in a tournament.

The first cricket World Cup was held in England in 1975 between the six test match playing nations plus Sri Lanka and East Africa. It is now held regularly every four years.

Rugby

The Rugby World Cup was not started until 1987. It was based in New Zealand and Australia. New Zealand beat France in the final. The second one was held in France and England and the third tournament in South Africa. This was South Africa's first chance to host a major championship since they had been re-admitted to world sport, and they celebrated by winning it. Each of the tournaments held has been bigger and more successful than the last.

Athletics

The first world championships in athletics were held in 1983 in Helsinki and were then held every two years from 1993. They alternate with the indoor championships which were first held in Paris in 1985 and are also held every two years. There are a great many athletics championships held throughout the world today.

There are separate ones for Africa, the Americas, the Caribbean, South-East Asia and the Arab States. There is even a World Student Games!

Specific matches and events

Some sports become international events because of the interest shown in a particular contest. This is often true with boxing, especially many of the heavyweight contests, which can attract huge international television audiences for the various versions of the world titles which are available.

Test match series, such as those played for in cricket and rugby, are also major events and can command a lot of attention.

The **Superbowl** is the climax of the American Football season when the final game is played between the winners of the two conferences (that is, the two separate leagues in America). It is billed as the world championship but is only open to American teams! It is also the most watched television event world-wide, ever broadcast!

Glossary

amateur someone who plays sport without being paid

apartheid a political system which was in force in South Africa. Apartheid discriminated against people because of their race or colour.

boycott refusing to attend an event as a form of protest

byes missing out on the opening round of a competition and going on to the next round automatically

chairperson the person in overall charge of a club

committee member person elected by the members of a club to run the club on their behalf

constitution the basic rules of how a club is run, which are accepted by all the members

controversial something that causes arguments and disagreements

de-motivates leads someone not to try so hard when competing

dieticians people who advise performers on their diet

dual provision where a school and a local community both use facilities at the same time

dual use where facilities are provided for school use during the day and community use at other times

etiquette an unwritten law or regulation in a sport, which is usually followed by the players or performers

extra-curricular activities any activities which take place in a school outside of set lesson times

GM Vauxhall Conference the football league which, at the time of publishing, was the next highest to the Football League

governing body the organization which runs and controls each particular sport

head-to-head final match played between the very best teams

host city the city chosen to be the venue for an Olympic Games

impartial an official who does not favour any one team or competitor over another

International Olympic Committee (IOC) the committee that, amongst other things, decides where the Games will be held

joint provision *see* dual provision

Jules Rimet one-time president of FIFA, after whom the first World Cup trophy was named

line judge person who checks that the ball stays within the allowed areas in a game such as tennis

local authority the local, or nearest government for a local area

match-up pairing up of different teams or players to take part in a competition against each other

member someone who belongs to a club

media television, radio or the press

minor official someone who is qualified to take responsibility for the less senior aspects of a sporting event

minutes a written record of an official meeting of a committee

national lottery weekly prize draw which raises money for good causes which include all aspects of sport

NCF National Coaching Federation

net cord judge the person responsible for checking that the net is kept at the right height, and that the ball passes clear of the net in a game such as tennis

neutral an official who does not come from either team or the same country or area as either team

officials people who organize or run sporting events

Olympic village houses or flats that are specially built for the athletes at the Olympic games to live in. Afterwards they may be used by the people living in the host country

open days days on which there is free access to clubs for non-members

open event a competition which can be entered by both amateur and professional performers

outdoor pursuits outdoor and adventurous activities

performance-enhancing drugs drugs that help someone perform better than they would if they did not take the drugs. Their use is against the rules.

physiotherapists experts who help to treat sporting injuries

plate competition a separate competition for first-round losers

play-off a tie-breaker where two well-matched players or teams hold a short competition to see who will be the winner

professional someone who is paid for doing a job or for playing sport

promoted put up to a higher division

qualified trained to act as an official at a sporting event

ranking position a position in a special list that is made up by checking how players of a particular sport perform and comparing them with each other

rarefied as applied to the atmosphere, thin and lacking in oxygen

relegated put down to a lower division

round stage in a competition

scouts staff from professional sports clubs who find and sign on young players or performers

season the times of year when a particular sport is played

secretary the person who does the paperwork, writes letters and prepares the minutes for a committee

seeded a player, or team, considered to be one of the best in any competition or tournament

semi-professional a sports player who gets paid for playing sport but who also works full or part time in another profession

senior official someone who has been trained or is experienced at the highest level, who can take on responsibility for running or judging a sports event

simulation a sporting situation which can be set up on a computer program

sin bin place where performers are sent to 'cool down' when temporarily sent off

sports psychologists experts who help to prepare sports performers mentally

subscription money paid every year for membership of a club

superbowl the final match of the American football season which decides the overall champion

surplus amount of money left over when all the bills have been paid

taster sessions free sessions to try out activities at clubs

travelling moving forwards when performing trampoline moves

treasurer person who deals with the finances of a club

umpire a person who oversees a match or game and makes sure that all the rules are followed

vice-chairperson the person who looks after things when the chairperson is absent

Wolfendon Gap loss of interest in sport after leaving school; this pattern of behaviour is named after the writer of a report which looked at why young people gave up sport after they left school

World Cup the world championship competition for soccer, played for every four years

Index